THE VOLUPTUARY

THE VOLUPTUARY

poems

Paulann Petersen

LOST HORSE PRESS
Sandpoint · Idaho

ACKNOWLEDGMENTS

A number of these poems (and some segments from sectioned poems) first appeared or are scheduled to appear in the following publications:

Basalt · *Bellingham Review* · *Birmingham Poetry Review* · *Burnside Review*
Chaffin Journal · *Clackamas Literary Journal* · *Cloudbank* · *Enigmatist* · *The Grove Review*
High Desert Journal · *Long Journey, Contemporary Northwest Poets*, edited by David Biespiel
Manzanita Quarterly · *National Forum* · *Notre Dame Review* · *Oregon Literary Review*
Porcupine · *RondeDance* · *South Carolina Review* · *Talking River Review* · *VoiceCatcher*

The book's third section, "The Hermaphrodite Flower," was published (with different sequencing) as a chapbook by Glenn Storhaug and Paul Merchant at Watzek Library Special Collections for the William Stafford Center, Lewis & Clark College.

"Small Wonder" was printed as a broadside by Berberis Press, Lewis & Clark College Special Collections.

"Bloodline" was printed as a letterpress broadside by Paper Crane Press, Half Moon Bay, California.

"To My Coffin Maker" was printed as a broadside by Tavern Books.

"Ember" was printed as a broadside by The Milwaukie Poetry Series.

Copyright © 2010 by Paulann Petersen
Printed in America.

Cover Art: Miri Lavee: "Pomegranates," oil on canvas, 30.8" x 57.7"
    Other fine art works by Miri Lavee can be viewed online at *www.art-miri.com*.
Author Photo: Sabina Samiee
    Photographs by Sabina Samiee may be viewed online at *www.sabinasamiee.com*.
Cover & Book Design: Christine Holbert

This and other LOST HORSE PRESS titles may be viewed online at *www.losthorsepress.org*.

FIRST EDITION

Library of Congress Cataloging-in-Publication Data

Petersen, Paulann.
The voluptuary : poems / by Paulann Petersen.
    p. cm.
ISBN 978-0-9844510-3-6 (alk. paper)
I. Title.
PS3566.E7636V65 2010
811'.54—dc22

                    2010028706

Leaves are not more shed from the trees, or trees from the earth,
than they are shed out of you.

—Walt Whitman

TABLE OF CONTENTS

I. A POWDER OF STARS

II. BLIND ABUNDANCE

V. THE SOMEWHERE OF BLUE

I

A POWDER OF STARS

Page not blank, but waiting,
sleep of a thousand
pale-lidded eyes, on you I leave
my telltale path, a blazing.

BLOODLINE

The moon is wet nurse
to roses. She suckles
each soft-mouthed poppy.

Blame her for menses.
Rail at her for the craving
to binge and purge.

Please her when you choose
to delay the day for planting,
biding your time
until night has fattened
her silver torso. Praise her
when the fleck of seed
poked down into damp dark
takes hold and swells.

Any girl-child is always
her offspring.

Upbraid her for your daughter's
sass and door-slams,
that hot hurry to be what most
differs from you.

Long ago, the moon decided
on a pathway against the route
stars take. No one else
would dare to walk
the black sky backward.

WHY THE WORLD ISN'T FLAT

Water would have no place
to travel. Rivers would have no beds.
Oceans, no ebb and go.

The stream you're beside
would have staggered and stymied
long ago. No fine rapids chatter.

Leafboats sailing along? Gone.
No downhill song
for former rain to croon.

No need for the fingerling trout
to make its swing-muscled
swim against the flow.

INDIGO

Blue bee, you hold
a sound in your body
so round, so flesh-bound,
its echo quivers
in spent expectation.

Piece of ether
caught and squeezed
to a single, blurred spot,
you're enough sky
to drone, to extrude wings.

Into housekeeping's cell
you loosen sugar
cool as a cast-off breeze,
blue honey so heavy
it buries a tongue.

Bee who gathers
the powder of stars,
you mark leaf, cloth,
and cheek with a smear
of upper air.

Thinking your dust
collected inside each iris
to give color to my eyes,
I was wrong.
Their blue is too tame.

But my throat is your hive,
its hum carousing
my veins. Excess, heat:
you rise from my skin,
a wavering shine.

FENNEL

The bird-plant spreads its feathers
to dry, its multitude
of bronzed green wings.

Many-winged phoenix, it reappears
from the soaked earth
each spring, bearing the underworld's

black-candy scent. Mantling in rain,
in wind—in sunlight, preening.
Only its seed will fly.

THIS COULD BE

pale ash falling in thick flakes
our burning city
being floated to pavement or

blood speckled on concrete
a neighbor's body blown apart
pied horror where we walk

it could   should   could be
war's numbing fallout
set into motion by black wings

but no   it's not
it's only blossoms   cherry and plum
falling   drifting

we wage war   yet live in peace
a crow stabs at the eddy of petals
again   we've been spared

SINCE MOST STARS ARE STRANGERS

Let a white hoop
    be the horizon.
Let fir trees
    wimple and gleam.
Let wind set up a tremor
    it never abandons.

Seven left eyes
    of seven crows
    wheel in a hubbub
    of dark jabber.
Wings overtake the day.

Let an elk take the sun
    away on its antlers.
    But only for a while.
Let the coat of a fox redden berries
    again, come summer.

Hope is that star whose place
    your eye can fix.
    You know it by name.
The largest room where you live
    calls itself *sky*.

WHAT'S LEFT FROM THAT FIRST GODDESS

Bits of her, finer than pollen,
still eddy the world with their dust.
Each speck of her makes
a seed for one of us.

Whole, where she lived in the sky,
her body contained all people, impatient,
straining toward birth.
She knew her huge self—
bone, brain, toenail and hair—
needed to crumble.

We are her, disassembled,
then grown into many.
We're the ones come from this First One
entirely broken apart, taken down
except for her mismatched eyes.

The right is a yellow
too bright to behold. The left,
a cool silver smudged
by cataracts of gray.
Our sun, our moon—
these, she saved.

ATAVIST

To conjure distance
merely wing it
make a straight
dark line
from here to there
and watch it glint
back at you.

As throwback
you accept no more
than the shortest length
a stone-black
wingbeat would take
to get from A to B—

no bigger
no beggarly less than
the exact way that
raven-kin forever
and after their arrival
here on earth
have gone about
their business
of being nothing
if not direct.

Just that far.

A WAY TO SAY GLADNESS

You can say *door.* You can say
the space the door divides,
empty space that thanks the door
for swinging on hinges inside it,
making of it two empty spaces,
a *this* and a *that,* a choice.

Or *hinges.* To bear the weight
of wood swinging from them, hinges
require screws biting into the jamb's wood.
Call the air moved by all this motion
a world's easy breath.

When greed sends you out and about,
a door will close enough to keep you
separate from what you crave.
As you walk away, look behind that door
one last time to note
what you wanted so badly.

The sigh you hold in will be
deep as a desert's well. Let it go.
Your next breath takes back
a bit of that sigh you loosed into air,
what was—a heartbeat ago—
your envy and dismay. Exhale
one of the hundred ways to praise.

IN FEBRUARY'S FIELD

Last fall's dull stubble
blunts the sheen of new grass.
Canada geese—too many to count—
sway-step across the prickle.
Feathered dun, they eye the ground
for a beetle, sow bug, beetle,
a sun-sodden fly. At field's edge

a startle: the white
of spectral skin. The lost daughter
rises again from below,
her fingers having broken through
the mat of roots and chaff.
Stunned for a moment by sharp air,
Persephone's hands
emerge in the form of one, two
bright swans. Day will be longer.
An underworld's darkness
sunders, falling away.

WHAT REMAINS

In a city of now,
fewer and fewer birds.
Mainly sparrows, robins.
Loss, only loss.

A grief—sharp and true.
Yet the sparrow is a *finch,*
thick-beaked weaver.
A robin, the storybook's *thrush.*

The crow is ever
raven and magpie's cousin.
Shape-changer, thief—
cobbled from black dust.

◇◇◇

Dusk-feeders tilt the day,
send it spinning on its axis.
Swing, veer, try as it might,
day cannot shake them away.
Dusk-feeders hang
upside down, grip the bottom
of the lurching, buckling
dwindle-day. Tight.

Grappled to some last
light, those feeding at dusk
are blue, are slate. They grow gray
eating the seed that glows.

IN THE BOOK OF WAVES

The first page is a mirror
throwing reflection forth
into a twin, never pausing, making
smaller and smaller versions.

The second is a narcissus
white-edged, sharpened with
the salt of perfume.

A tongue counts as a third—
the sound of lapping lapping.

An egret offers
a wavelength of egress.
A stairway, a length of ascent.

Stars come to us in waves.
Theirs is a library
without end.

FOREVER FORBIDDEN TO WED

Marry up—
if you're lucky.
Marry down only if there's a way
not to tell your parents.
But how to marry across the distance
between day and night? How to wed
a drop of milk in the sky
when you're that golden colossus,
the Sun? No way.
So each dawn the Sun swallows
his love for the Moon
and shoulders along, alone.

The Moon never tires
of pining, of baring her mottled self
for all to see. She pretends
to be wearing her wedding shift
blotched with the faded
stain of maiden-blood.
In time, she convinces herself
the night sky has filled
with her grown children.
Poor creature. It's easy to see
how she might. Look how the Stars
resemble her beloved.
Look how they manage to keep
their distance from her.

IN A FLECK OF THE COSMOS

An ocean groans
its salt-belly,
dark and roiling.

Trees stitch
the earth to the sky.

Rivers are wings
sprung from a mountain's
white shoulders—
mantling out, down,
lit with glint.

Each lake, each pond
flicks a lazy tongue.

The sun proffers
reflection. The moon
leads us astray.

A gull makes itself
small enough to become
twin specks—

reflections on
the right, the left,
on each of our
twice grateful eyes.

SKIN

Between our two eternities of darkness,
what's to be done? Pick up the table knife
from the table's cloth and peel
an apple's skin from its wet flesh.

Your knife is not made for such work.
Its blade, not sharp to begin with,
is clumsy from all the butter it's spread,
the forcing of meat from bone.

And yet. With practice—
not even art, but simple-minded rote—
skin can be parted from its body
in one spiral of derring-do.

Given light and the slap of air,
flesh will yellow, rust,
scurry to brown.
Grow its own darkness.

II

BLIND ABUNDANCE

A heart is the body's flower,
its venture into dusk
and darkness, blind abundance
lasting through night.

Look how the heart makes a body
new, moment after moment—
each beat a going-to-seed,
a growing-back from the same.

SKY-SOWER

Scattering it freely,
in handfuls I throw the sky about.
A sower, I arc the seed lying

so close at hand it's colorless:
sky-seed so far from the blue
above, it's clear.

Easy it scatters, not up
or down, but made of air and thus
everywhere. Letting me hold it,

mother it, pull long, round
cushions of it into my lungs.
Croon, skim, ruffle it,

lurch. The sky scattered low
into breath. Words skidded across
my teeth and tongue.

Blue horsetail of words. Blue
flames, hordes, the hoarded
blue of unopened song.

DOXOLOGY

I believe in the one flesh,
single body, all appetites
visible and indivisible,
in hunger without end.
The tongue will find its mote
of honey, the nose its meandering
musk. The ear will fill
and empty and be full again
with song—dry cave, drinking.

◇◇◇

No way to touch
and not have what I touch
touching me. Green glass
seethes with light, drinks it
into an emerald throat.
I touch it, and under that spot,
light is gone.
                    Green moon-glass
meets my skin
with its dark side—
leaf-splurge, grass-glare
covered by the fleshy tone
bounced back at my eyes
from my fingertip.

Moonlight of any night
finds me, its pewter
sutures my face. I write
the poems of every other,
every poet writes mine

ASHES

Because we call the body
ashes, dust,
clothing. Containment.

Because each word
is a body-print—
dark home of indelible ink.

Because a poem breathes
air into this world,

I am here to stuff
my limbs with leaves—
ready to be

the scarecrow of
a thousand
green say-so's.

EMBER

Let the sun rise and set
farther and farther south.
Let the days faster and faster
shrivel into dusk.
Sometimes my eyes work
on the fine world's print,
mostly not. Still,
each breath is a revelation
I've not breathed before.

This morning-come-lately,
the sun lobs a tree's
whole shadow-self against
an outer wall. Each leaf gives its
swaying sideshow of *Yes, let wind
pass through me,* or *No,
not yet, not now.*

A wind means one thing's
heating up, while another cools,
in uneven rate. I am *another,*
cooling down, click by
unsteady click—a last fever
lodged at the tip of my tongue.

BRIGHT SONG BRED IN A DARK THROAT

These singing birds are wholly black,
might be both white
and black. *Magpie,* I say,
knowing such creatures can copy
any voice, can claim
each bird's song. Crow's cousin,
raven's kin, overgrown
relation to these birds of mere darkness,
they chortle in fields nearby.
Aware a magpie wouldn't be caught
dead in this garden, I wish
a flock of them here. All the same.
I wish my mother alive.

She thrilled to bone china.
Her nurse's hand—
all too acquainted with blood—
lifted a saucer into light.
Finding a sun to back up
her claim—*You can see
right through it*—
fingers of her left hand
fanned out behind the china to show
a gray ghost. Her hand
not even that shadow-maker now.

A blackbird throat
spouts yellow back at the light.
Call it song. My mother has become
a shade. She resides behind and under
whatever stops the sun's light,
living somewhere
between white and black—
a gray flightless bird.

In sun streamed with birdsong,
I still make—I've not yet become—
a stolid, coal shadow.
No light finding its way through me.
I watch for magpies, to stray.

Whose bones are ground
fine enough to become a porcelain
inviting light to pass straight through?
My mother's reduced themselves
to the bits in her ashes,
mix of white and gray—
box of ashes I've kept these thirteen years
since her death. In dark letters
a label states her name, in full.
I don't know the tune for
Farewell, Disperse
when so little remains.

No song without the bird's night
gleaming along its back and wings.
Both light and shade,
the magpie holds enough white to make
a small star shine. Enough
black to swallow
a sun whole.

Mother-may-I, save me
from a giant step, from birds
too much of one
non-color or the other. Spare me
from having to claim either
black or white.
How could I learn to grind
a bird bone, something so hollow
it's mostly air? I eat
from plates of clay. My only song
makes itself from an earth
thinned by ash.

PROPAGATE

Every seed Abundance sheds
makes a flower. Every and each.
Take this blossom called night
sucking the last of day
through its blue-violet straw.
Or the river—it's surely one—
that loosely wound clock running out.
Whatever bit of herself Abundance sows
grows into a vessel filling
with her sharp perfume.
Every last thing's been first
her body, her seed
and desire, then some flower
given away to bloom in her
spendthrift world.

Include the power line
humming its double-fisted tune.
An icehouse stacking up
the loose change of winter's regret.
A downspout hemmed
to the house, its empty throat
wide and waiting. Count it all.
Note the fox. Mostly reckon
the vixen prickling inside
her bottlebrush of fire.

SPAN

What my hand learns, my heart
already knows. What—for an instant
of its longingful life—I grasp
between thumb and finger's whorling
cushions, grows too in my core:
each sprout, each twig,

any handful of earth pressing
its faint sour molding of leaf,
sweet decay into my palm's own
plumped furrows.
The *anywhere*-skin's
touch comes out of the heart

and its endlessly-soon-to-be-ended
beating. A hand's stroke, its hold,
are the blood's tingle, its recognition
of hard, succulent, *world*.
Unhinged and hinged, the bending.
Every hand. Its one wild heart.

THE LIGHT CONNECTING EACH TO ALL

On wooden siding, the leaf's
shadow is a self
and that self's twin ghost.

A little breeze shakes the leaves,
their shadows, both
sun-fed forms.

Shine and quake: a thousand
green heartbeats now colorless,
as good as transparent.

A tree's repeating systoles
now spread across the painted wood.
A side of my house, alive.

✧✧✧

A plank of bright, honeyed wood
surrounded by others
weathered and aged.
A brand-new board
made from a golden body
laid down among the dark ones
in an old deck outdoors.

This freshly-cut shaft of tree
is the work
of the sun—its one
light growing all light. I see
this yellow board and *see*.
A line of pollen touches
each leaf, every mouth
to the mouth of a bee.

What moon has my lifted hand
circled in the hoop of finger and thumb—
the sign for perfection—
and not held? What stem of a daffodil in bud
has it pierced apart with thumb
and index nail, and then not grasped—
with lymph falling in clear strings—
a star bursting?

To a goddess of uncountable beauty,
many hands are given; to a monster chained
beneath the ancients' earth, eight dozen more.
From someone blamed—the one merely human—
a hand can be taken back, severed away.

Little tool, heart's prehensile,
seize this world for me.

THE MILKY WAY

My thumbnail severs
the lettuce plant's stalk,
its acrid milk flung in a path
of shining drops across
dark soil as I carry the leaves
off to be washed, chilled,
torn and eaten.

The Virgin Mother uncovers
one breast so a master painter
can depict this world—
how milch-stars spray light
from her nipple.

Night lets down the galaxy,
a nacre-white stream.
On a map's *You are here,* the *here*
is less than a speck in the swath
made from dying or forming suns,
gasses, and dust. What seems
to lie far beyond
cradles us.

My breasts, slack.
Decades ago, hungry for
whatever thin, bluish food

they could suck from me,
my children sloughed off
then replaced each of their
own cells. My babies nursed
and became something else,
themselves anew.
The way of milk.

BE HERE WHEN I CAN SEE YOU, WHEN I CAN'T

Stars, you are the heavens' flock,
tangling your pale wool across
the night sky, bits of oily fleece
catching on barbs of darkness to swirl
in black wind. You appear, disappear
by thousands, scattered wide to graze
but never straying. While I—a mere
shepherd of these words—am lost.

What can I do but build a small blaze,
feed it with branches the trees let fall—
that twiggy clatter strewn along the ground.
Lichen crusting such dead limbs
glows silver, white. Earth-food for a fire
so unlike and like your own.

AMONG THE YET UNFALLEN

Last night with eyes shut down
by dark, I passed under
an orange tree's branches.
The perfume that fit
its succubus mouth over my face
breathed into me
its yellow oil.

Morning, and the musk joins
sunlight in a journey to the patchy grass
under this tree whose leaves
and year-old oranges
do not drop—the scent joined
by a steady contralto of bees
black as the blossoms are white.

Bees sing their darkness
from flower to flower.
In this cosmos of leftover orange planets,
the black stars feed on the white.

III

THE HERMAPHRODITE FLOWER

A Father, you are, Walt Whitman. And I, grass-child to your tree
    whose leaves as you wrote them
    saw ahead to the me bearing your name.
You, great oak, fir, Father Larch to this leaf of grass,
    my leaves growing scattered, but green
    and skyward under your spread-forth shade.
Praise be to you and your eyes that found me.
Praise your soul bounding ahead.

NEARNESS CALLED FORTH

Thoughts hugely swollen with song
fell down upon you as you walked
under trees needing no blossom
beyond the bloom of your eyes,
your stride, your boot's sole slaking
the pathway. Oh, the gravity called forth
by your nearness: weightless songs
given their heft at your passing,
ripeness brought down from branches.

Groves sprouted and arbored
to await the day, that hour
you happened along.
                    For you, even
the fruitless tree bore sweetness.

❖❖❖

That big and handsome moth
you knew—not by name
but by sight and touch—
lit so your extended hand
could hold him.

Did you trust your arm
out into openness?
Tremored with field and woods,
did he seek you out?
Who waited, you or he?

Maybe your handsome fellow
was a carpenter moth,
his doubled wings the sable's
brown summer coat. His body
thumb-thick and ruffled with scale.

Perhaps he knew you
by scent—old-man fusty beard,
deep-creased skin,
your fingers smeared by
their recent coupling
with grease and bread.

◇◇◇

For you came to know
yourself as ocean. Both
cradler and source
of the river you once
supposed yourself to be.
For you were spume, scud,
mist and cloud, downpour
percolated through humus and rock
to well up again, flowing.

How can I then—
in this *then* living now—
heed the canon *less is more*
and hesitate? For you
emptied out of and into
yourself—ocean and river
bearing one mouth. No excess
too large for embrace.

VANTAGE

Night-piece I carry with me
every sunlit day,
the little darkness moving
however I do, absence leaping
quick as movement itself.
Infallible mime, shadow perfumed
with iron, a struck match. Sawdust
rotting into heat, but cooler
nonetheless. My weightless body
clad in black, thrown down.

Tell me, Father, where will I be in a day,
a week, next year, when the sun no longer has me
to interrupt its journey to earth? Will you too
disappear? What other darkness will touch
the ground at every step when I
no longer step? Only a flame
throws no shadow—only memory,
flame, this written breath.

✧✧✧

I live in your fine hodge-podge,
my soul alongside yours.

Beside that of a rooftop's slant,
of angled rain skittered down

window panes. A crutch I tuck
under my arm's hollow

hobbles me along. Extra leg,
dull gleam of limb.

Parts toward an expanding soul
cobble themselves together by touch.

By need. By a craving
to walk this world.

◇◇◇

I see how your grass spreads out to grow.
How, after a skyward shoot to crumble dirt aside,
    it sidles for a while,
opens like the goddess' many arms,
    curving to enfold,

many-armed grass, many-handed leaves,
and at each juncture, multiples—
    no blade a loneliness for long,
alone for only a moment before
    growth goes on becoming.

I keep my sight at ground level.
Many are the orphan stars your grass
    takes into its embrace.

ONE SOUL

When I wrap my legs around
the moon, drawing it toward my core,
will I be filled and satisfied?

When I leave my smudge of musk
on its skin, my name's perfume
beside your name—

O Life-Caresser—will I be
silent then? When I ride the moon,
hips spread, thighs astraddle,

rolling its weight under me,
side to side, succulent golden grape
grown huge enough

to fit my body's love, will I then
be flinging light backward
at a star's absent face?

Not my face, its features,
imprint of smile or frown.
Not this brain toting
its bundle of laundry

aired on the line
of speculation and regret.
Not the rapid-firing
yes and no of what I know,

but the body of which
face and brain are only part.
One that knows in its
inarticulate parts how much

it owes to one
immensely larger. Worthy
of you, your largesse.
The universe within.

◇◇◇

Let me stand by your side
and with you look
into a mirror, watching your eyes
gazing back at our selves.

Forward and into the past.
Back at the days ahead
contained in your own reflection,
in your line-sprawled pages.

Two of you. This one whose warmth
leans into my shoulder, whose
deep-taken breathing my own
follows. This other around
whose mirror-image I can see
all that stands just behind us.

HERMAPHRODITE

The poppy, hermaphrodite.
Female and male, both at its hub.
The pistil's sticky womb
topped by a seven point crown.
Anthers wobbling to cast
that soft rain of yellow sperm.
The root-reach into an underworld
concoursed by worms.
The rise—head bowed, nodding—
toward a none-too-distant star.

Each day of May as you
hobble-scuffed along that path
from farmhouse to creek,
you were the hermaphrodite flower.
Gathering as you went
a turbid aura of wild bees.

✧✧✧

Your shirt's turned-down collar
vast, wide, at times
edged with lace

but open, always open,
its top button no higher than
your breastbone.

White linen wings
spreading under the gray
moss of your beard.

Throat and chest
allied with fits of sun, wind.
Untied, ever untied.

◇◇◇

Your beard rinsed twice
in sun, lofted by wind,
whitened by a moon's ministration.

You who christened yourself
Cheapest Nearest Easiest
are the maker who calls sacred
whatever your voice might touch.

Holy are those salts, those oils
that rose to live on your skin.

Holy the pores that held them.
Sweat, gloss, dander, rime.

Holy the tongue whose tip
was given that glint to taste.

NUMEN

For your long-lined pages,
their white leaves
veined with darkness,
you saw readers without end.

No end to life as we may
or may not know it.
A stream of work-chafed hands
to open your book.

Voices to read aloud
your poem not of land alone,
but astride the shoreline,
one foot in sea, one not.

Your poem, the ocean's
slip-slack, flow and going.

◇◇◇

One day you re-christened yourself
the *Half-Paralytic.* Your body indeed
half-rigid, but as a tree's half
is rigid. Roots fixed,
trunk upright, steady.

Only branches bending
and buckling in wind.
Only leaves skittered, torn,

thrown to the ground
to be ground into duff.

Sucked in, then lifted up
again—into leaves.

◇◇◇

Let me grow within
your tree's axis, my roots
looped firm into shale and silt,
my heart given the honesty
only a dumb and chambered
muscle can have.
Large enough to pump
my vegetable lymph up and up.
Clear blood ascending
until each finger
of my ten thousandfold hands
unfurls itself—green
net to snare the sun.

RESERVOIR

For you, the sky dropped—into its
lowest reaches—a remedy.
Medicinal air and light,

weightless, wandering.
No boundary for it, not even
the shell, bark or bedrock

of another. Whoever would be
hermetic would need each seam
sealed by a wildwood of pitch.

Open, you said—
loose-clothed, loose-skinned.
Let the sky in.

At midsummer's midnight you stood
outside to hear wingbeats make
a deep, uneven current overhead.
Songbirds, shorebirds in migration.

Voices. A reedy plink, high-pitched
creak, whistle-wheeze.
Bobolink, thrush, tanager, plover,
for three hours above you.

Now and again, a clear carol—
tyeep, tut-tut-tut
tyeep, tut-tut-tut.

◇◇◇

Into a brook,
to write your lines,
you dipped a *water-pen*—

tiny stick of ink
dissolving inside the pen's
reservoir you filled
so you could empty
and fill it again.

Your handwriting's
bold meander, a stream.
Gurgling, limpid
inseparable from
making and maker.

No need to carry
along on outings
a bottle of the poem's
dark blood. All around,
earth's great heart
goes beating.

IV

SOUNDING-BOWL

How sturdy, this going-on world.
How necessarily incomplete
its ongoing push to complete itself.

ARK

Shape of the sun's own
roundness, of a mid-cycle moon
poised at the peak
of its path through night.
A filling, fully glass bowl
floating into this room.
Round ark that holds
the whirl of yin and yang—
every creature's
dark and light aboard.

I circle one fingertip,
gleamed with spittle, along
the bowl's rim.
My tongue has wet
my body's only whorled skin,
so this imprint of me
can brush against
a never-ending edge.
Half a globe. *Hollow.*
From its pole I hear
an underworld drone.

FIG

Half dried, half not. Skin puckered.
Your stem-end curves directly
into your golden-bronze body
scabbed here and there
with sugar so brash
it oozes out.

I *do care a fig* for you,
soft pouch of sweetmeat
that grew beside leaves
a hundred times your size.
To tear you open reveals
a sticky bed of glistening seed.
To bite, to chew, is to grind—
against my teeth—
a sun's fine grit.

FEEDING CROWS

I can move closer. Too much,
and they scatter. Snap and clatter of black
lifted to trees. Caw and creech railing at intrusion.

Of late, my heart startles, flying against my chest.
Aberrant beats, thousands each day. Panicked,
I tell it, *I must tame you to survive.*

No. I'll give this dark nester
what it craves. Sleep
laden with dreams. Then—from a distance—

morsels of fond neglect.

A PINCH OF YOUR ASHES
MIXED WITH MOTHER'S

Pressing what I can
between fingertip and thumb,
I drop them into the Seine.
Bits of bone—yours dark, hers light—
fall into water. A pale film
floats in air rising
from the current's hurried gleam.
Maybe this updrafted powder
finds its way down into river-brim,
maybe it drifts
up into my breath.

I'm near Notre Dame's stone lacework—
a cathedral Mother would have
swooned to, church you might have
affably admired.

How easy, Father—with you two
dead this long, me getting
closer all the while—how simple
to carry a bit of you
with me, here to France.

Bosphorous, Black, Arabian. These are seas
I've sprinkled with your ashes.

Ayder, Orontes, Seine. Three rivers
I've asked to bear you away.

Every current brings
you back. Each rain is both itself
and a freshet, then a stream
headlong becoming a river feeding
this ocean that's us. I breathe
you toward me. In each swallow
of sweet water, I taste
your fine, mineral trace.

FAR

At my table's center I've set
a lotus blossom, its red petals
made from translucent shell.
No stamen, pistil, or anther.
At its heart, a candle flame
rises to eat from the air
each of my overgrown sighs.
I breathe beeswax and heat.

Refusing—on any one day—to be
washed away, bits of yesterday
carry forward. My mouth's corner
forms a crust—the grain and grit
of sweetness grown old.

Somewhere, a woman spoons
honey made by bees who spurn
feeding on anything save
lotus blooms. A place
not impossibly far.

FOR CONTINUANCE

Pray that blood
still flows, and after
three days or four
the bleeding ceases of its
own accord. Pray an egg—
tiny glister-moon—
rises to enter
a replenished womb.
Pray for a spurt
of whip-tailed stars.
May they shoot like crazy
through dark to reach
that drop of waiting light.

SILVER & DEEP

Drinking the water today's sun
bathed in, I reel and stammer,
chasing whatever the wind
throws my way, breathing
big to clear my hazing eyes
until this walking-level world feels
more ordinary and organized,
the weight of my feet on dirt
and concrete nothing more
than me, pressing down.

But the sky's on the loose,
rain clouds bustling
across its skin fast as they can.
I quick swallow a draft
the moon bathed in, tasting a stream
overgrown with oaks. Leaves steep
soothing tannin into the flow—
yellow tea brewed from trees who are
the moon's familiars here on earth.

Fine as any line-up of suns
a night sky could flaunt,
this dipper deepens.
My drinking gourd shines.

APPEAR

A yellow chair says yes
to blue. With braced legs
and canted arms, it embraces
as much sky-hue as it can bear,
soaking it in. Each surface atom's
a mouth made to swallow blue,
a snub-buzz sending yellow
straight back to my eyes—
this chair called by exactly
what it's not drenched in,
named for what its skin repels.

I'm called white because my skin
swims in blackness. My hair was dark
only because it guzzled too much
light. My eyes—having welcomed
yellow for a lifetime—are nothing
if not pale blue. Every color I see
comes from rejections suffered
by light. My eyes are on the lookout
for a blue so pure I can carry it
to another world—sky enough
to fill muscle and marrow,
weight my swelling heart.

ABANDON

Its nostrils, the soft of a rabbit's kindle.
Its rump, two globes grown
in an orchard owned by the pale moon.
Coat, the mayhem of never-mind.
With all effect, no cause, a horse
galloped the nearby field's outer edge,
rounding its hard geometry.

My upper arm heated
where I'd careened into a doorframe
getting better position to see.
At any single moment I had
free for looking out,
I checked that field—
small triangle of quack grass
across the driveway. The horse
was either there, or not.
Mostly not. Younger then,
I watched more, saw less.

A bruise gathered color, beginning
its swim to the surface. Day was raw,
the field unkempt, my discontents
a bare breath away. In a short week,
the bruise had made entry and exit.
My complaints—and the sorrow
they later pushed forth—those took years.
I could list them all now
only because long ago
I memorized their names.

I've forgotten the bruise's touchiness,
too much like too many that followed.
The bleak vista from home is gone.
But *that horse.* My eyes open, each breath
a food for the sight that took the creature in.
A heart raced to race an animal's
lightened weight round and round.
No purpose, no need. That remains.

YET AGAIN I NAME ALOUD

the linchpins of this world:
Fir pollen. Birch pollen.
Their yellow drift.
Willow pollen—meandering
the ground in eddies
supple as the branches
letting it go. I mustn't leave
catkin unsaid. *Cone,* either.

I'd like to have been the one
who dreamed up *birch*
and—after touching its pale,
curling husk for luck—
first spoke it into the world.
Some lucky one got to make up
fir and *willow,* too.

Then *magnolia,* the first
true flower. Wobbling anthers,
sticky pistil. Evolution's brazen move.
Magnolia pollen. There, it's said.
The body of this world
puts on its coat of wild color,
arms alive with waving.

GRAVITY

Owned by the stars, I dare not
wish them any closer.
Star-bred, the mole, that gouger,
knows not to stray from earth.

Mud clings to feet, reveals
the moist arch under claw and nail.
What the body expels
is buried in plosive—

dirt, dank. Even blood,
once out, turns first
to rust, sees its precocious glare
sink to teeming black.

✧✧✧

The sun would do its murder
of me, the moon too,
if I were not a smallest sun,
were not an even slighter
moon-home for its lent light.

The wind would come
to tatter me away, suck
my lungs empty of air
if my breath did not create
its own humid breeze.

Surely rain would fill
and drown me. For certain,
except for this wellspring
of words—enough that they
fall on each open place.

✧✧✧

No blowse of heart,
lungs, stomach and bowel, no little
eddies of fat-sunk skin: the *understated*
is skeleton only, blameless
in its retrospect. Opal-clean bones
and tooth-clenched skull. No bulk
of the possible words, their possible stink.

Yet flesh is what I know—
its less than cautious voice.
And doesn't a skeleton
take its very shape
from the left-unsaid's shadow weight?

I leave understatement to the gods,
leave its clacket of bones to my burial dirt.
Blown too human, I praise, I sing.

DEATH-CLOTHES

I'd need a summer death, early fall at the latest.
Then some swiftly working seamstress could stitch together
large leaves from my garden's plume poppies—
each leaf turned downside up
so its underbelly furred with silver shows.
A last dress of green moonlight.

Or any season in the not too near future,
my body could be rolled across countless butterfly wings—
me, turned and turned, until iridescence
became the garment for blue-hearted flames to take.
The lone monarch I years ago found dead
and have kept—a darkness windowed with orange—
it could be a start.

One fall day, not so long ago,
I learned. Burial clothes can be
almost anything other than Sunday-best.
Polite strangers zipped my mother into a plastic pouch—
a black cocoon that moved from the shifting
shine of her limbs as they
carried her out.

MOONFLOWER

crimping tendrils
cordate leaves
of deepened green

spiral buds
waiting to loosen
at fallen dusk

the one destined
to bloom
apart from day

this very night
a ghost blossom
unfurls against

blue-black air
one trumpet of
unearthly perfume

one winding
of pale grave-cloth
now unwound

the sun's
dark mirror
at last undone

WHOSE FEET I'D DRY WITH MY HAIR

My mother's. Her left foot drawn up,
a crooked and knotted claw-foot
made by a break when she was a child.
No doctor. No plaster for a cast.
Too much trouble, too little cash.
Often I gazed with her at the Sirens
in shoe store windows downtown.
All her grown life she longed to wear
those open, thin-strapped high heels.
I wash and dry her left foot
a second time.

Your feet, Walt Whitman.
Even though you seem preoccupied,
barely noticing what dries
your yellowed, uncut toenails.
But you hear me say we're kin,
we share a last name. *Shared,* you chide,
reminding me I gave mine up
to marry, asking why I dye my hair dark,
why not leave it gray, like your own?
Into your jacket pocket I slip—beside
a plover feather you've kept from your walk
on Long Island shore—these leaves
I've written to you.

The feet of a black-crowned night heron.
This time I'm lucky dye covers my gray.
The bird notes some kinship,

lets my hair dry its long claws
still wet from wading Link River.
With a steely beak, the heron reaches over
to rip a bit of dark hair from my scalp—
rooted in silver, speckled with blood,
strands it will weave into its nest.

TO MY COFFIN MAKER

Make me a wooden coffin,
one to house my body above ground
on a far-flung, wind-scoured place.

Use boards already weathered,
wide and old. Pine. Dimension lumber
you're not likely to find in the fresh stacks
of some resin-scented yard.

Raised grain, warps,
a popped knot or two: all OK,
as long as it has that silver,
water-rubbed finish of age.

Shape the box itself
as you like. Just remember: 5' 8,"
wide shoulders, long-toed feet.

I want two uprights
bolted to the coffin's sides—
one to the right, one to the left,
aligned with a line
that would pass through my chest.

These are perches, for birds
I'll also have you make.
Two coffin-birds of a type
that might nest in the pines.

Carved feathers, carved claws.
No paint. No stain.

Make the first with its beak
open. The other, shut.

One for song,
one for the quiet after.

V

THE SOMEWHERE OF BLUE

Threshold, hinge,
machine of transformation—
may the great door swing.

ANTHEM

Erotic thrum sounds
the names of this world.
Water, anther, belly.
Seed, stripling and *sun.*

Not merely our sex, no.
Never a *that* or a *this* only.
But earth's sex, the all
of binding and flying away.

Honey hugged to six walls.
Pollen falling from laden
haunches. All wings, all
coupling, the pull of every
each to an each.

Whole, this world
is the bees' work—flowers,
fodder, milk, meat,
all creatures, feeding.

I want to become
the work of their mouths—
beeswax filled, emptied,
each of my sides

shared with another. Oily,
viscous, sweet with esters.
Meadow-fumed,
ready to flame.

SMALL WONDER

The robin can hear a worm
move underground—earthworm
eating a channel through dirt.

She tilts her head as if she could
lie on her side and press
an ear to the ground.

She is dun, yes, but a breeze riffles
her feathers so pale down shows through.
Her eye is ringed.

A black bullseye encircles
what is already black as a midnight pond—
a target that draws eyes to her eye.

She is redbreasted, no. Not really.
Her chest is a red softened,
made light—the pale of a milkless breast.

What milk she has she keeps
deep in her body: that white surrounding
each egg's heavy core.

A yolk the color and shape of the sun
feeds a hatchling that becomes
the shape and color of her.

No wonder she can hear—
moving in the world beneath—
what must eat the earth to live.

WATERMELON

Summer's tri-colored flag
stitched with black stars—
each a state in the union
of sugar and water—
your sweetness allies
finger to finger,
makes fingertips a magnet
for the tongue.

No shriveler, no shrinking
grape or plum, you're
the river's apple,
a rain-sotted gourd—

willing to burst open
of your own accord
if left unpicked too long.
Inside you, day turns
heat into a pink mead

so we can drink
the sun and be drunk.

SOLAR ECLIPSE

In case of murder—
some devil or dragon devouring
the sun—make a racket
of wails and whooping shouts.
Bang on copper plates
you've polished to mirrors.
Send enough hubbub out and up
to scare the demon into
dropping its prey.

Then again, it could be *love:*
the moon's legs wrapped around
the sun's thick hips.
In case of such a mating—heat
escaping their locked bodies,
that visible ring of flares
huge in the sky—
don't even yip. Play it safe.
Look the other way.

HEAVENLY BODY

Hair unwound, reaching
down to her knees.
Breasts small, nipples pale.
Naked but for a feral crown of roses.
In her left hand, a loose
woodland bouquet.
Her polished mirror in the right.
Painted onto a parchment page
of a 15th century book,
Venus, the Evening Star.

Below her, a half-circle
of poplars making a backdrop
on the earthly stage. Two lovers
posed in front of the curve
of trees, their faces leaning
close enough to mix breath.
A player strumming his lute.
Three swains wooing a Lady.
None of them yet looking up
to find Venus already smiling
above the horizon's curve.

Soon enough they'll spy
the star-gleam itself—
those golden rays streaming
from their hub,
the delta of her sex.

Of course she smiles.
From the time she first
spread her legs wide and held
a mirror to herself, she understood.
Labial light. What shines
from between her thighs
masters the night.

HIVE

The bee notes every moment.
Takes notice from a thousand cousins
of each veer and rise
to the hive. Lets go its own
dusted scent bit by bit.
By its flurry makes—later
to spend—more esters,
now and now.

Shudder and thrum,
scent accreting. Blur and blunder,
scent cast off to mark
where the bee has been.

Flowers are named for what
they bring—another flower's
sex and bluster.
Whichever way enough
have traveled—that becomes
the path home.

WAX

Prairie, meaning *meadow,*
makes a stream of breath
rising toward the sky as if
to tell of grassland bearing
the makings for a pale brew.

Mead came early, from a sound-stem
meaning *honey,* itself even older
and shaped in the mouth to mean
golden, that mother of words.
Prairie speaks of grasses

flowered and bent by pollen,
a sweetness thinned with water
and left to ferment.
Meadow is drunk, yellow-laden,
the day's weighted bee.

The body once took with itself
beeswax into the grave. Once dead,
a body was wrapped in fabric
stiffened by wax. *Cerecloth.*
Coat, and its own coating.

Bee-makings hot then dripping,
carried along. The great strum,
the need to enter and leave

sex's yellow dust.
Pale light taken under.

The stubborn body wound itself
with sun. Wrap of orchard,
bloom-pocked weeds, taken down.
Melted into warp and weft,
this balm of the quick.

MEND

wounded and pierced
even the animal called *night*
will heal

although not straight-away
not without leaving
indelible marks

our eyes wander
the velvet pelt
of darkness above

stars are a sky's
proud flesh
its hard sidereal scars

ON THE ONE TRUE WAY
OUT OF THIS WORLD

I awoke today having slept with Death.
You heard what I said. The spot
where Death's body and mine had spooned
still gave off warmth.

Death is a tree. Tall, limber column. Dark leaves dusted
with the underworld's ash.
My bed sheets gleam with a trace
of its grit. So I sleep with a tree now and then. So what.
Don't pretend it's simple. You know
a little something about Death.

It's a bird. Nocturnal. What else to expect?
Hollow-boned raptor. Eyes big enough to suck in
the least bit of light.
A creature who coughs up
balls of fur and bone. I sleep with that.

I breathe in styptic, old creosote,
taste lavender in my breath. Somewhere in Death's shadow,
my father rambles on about dimension lumber.
Straight-grained, kiln-dried, clear.
Mother sings in tongues.
Her bridge club, who trumped what.
It's their rapture of sorts.
They've been dead too long.

Mornings, I rub my eyes
and feel the sting of copper under my lids.

Death is a scythe, a stain. Crescent blade
I curve against. Of course I try to be careful.
I get nicked now and again,
but there's so little blood, no one's apt to notice—
unlike those well-deep blotches
once soaking my bedclothes each month.
You're thinking *the moon,*
but the moon isn't Death. You know better.

Now I discover Death is the sister
of Sleep. Imagine that. Don't pretend you didn't
realize all along. I gain the siblings I've always wanted,
didn't have. Never mind. It's late
and my fingers dig in, taking root in familiar night.
We twine together, arms enwrapped.
Death and Sleep and me. A family.

CRESCENTS

Bits of the body drift to earth
in pale crescents, gibbous flecks.

Shed, shed—the body falling away
from itself, yet whole and growing.

Bits rubbed off, sloughed,
pared away. Gleaming.

New moons left behind—
cast into constellations of grass.

WICK

Ladder of bark, branching stilt, a tree
defies all gravities by straining
upward to draw and drink.

As much out of sight as in, it taps
the netherworld's cistern to spray
foliage across the scrape of sky.

A lily pistil oozes at its stigma,
drop-dropping the glistering glue of sex
it sucks out of garden's bed.

A bee—its mouth part dipped into honey,
wing-blurred body rising to the sun—
siphons amber back toward its source.

Each craver candles forth a glad flame.
Leaves tongue a green blaze, the wax
of such fire dripping down taper-trunks.

Thin treacles of sap give back
what a tree's yellow thirst
drew from the seething ground.

THE METAMORPH WORLD

Never-green, new growth is yellow,
gold, chartreuse—something else growing
into green. On one tree, what's new
unfurls into leaves
breakaway red.

Whatever our eye beholds
it tries to hold still. Go slow,
slower, the eye cries,
but the red of this tree's bursting nodes
is a flicker that sight can only
try to contain.

Foliage, foil, roil, flame
hold the shudder, the shimmer, because
words don't hold still.
Wells of sound, words travel and dip
from *limb* to *limbo, leaf* to *leave,*
red to *ready,* already going to *green.*

FOREST SUTRA

All night a great tree
grows under the stars' tutelage.
Day long, it grows beneath
the teaching of a single star.

Its conifer eyes learn to recite
the lesson *green*—each
glistening pupil
dark with resin-perfume.

✧✧✧

A forest steadies
itself by being
spirit, by becoming
thread. Each tree

a stitch, a rooted
link to the heavens—
the sewing that joins
earth to air.

Along thick, sidling
limbs, the dead
of a long-lost people
were laid. Face up.

Eyes closed,
they turned to that place
where a tree-top
fastens to sky.

A woodstove's chimney looses
shape-shifters upward.
A fine, white ribbon
rolls into a vaporous feather
that buckles.
Roiling wisps widen
enough to disappear.

With their embrace,
smoke-limbs reach so high,
so wide, they fly apart
into being what they are not.
The sky, all this *sky*:
here, above us,
the tree's
last ghost.

CROWS FEEDING ON CRUSTED SNOW

Hands of the night, the crows
have arrived here to feed
on long-gone heat, to pluck
summer from winter's white cloth.
They feed on bread thrown
atop fallen snow. On wheat's fruit.
On what pale dust the millstones
crushed into being. On the work of an oven,
smallest sun sealed in a cave.

These shadows have cut themselves free
from night's body. They are extremities,
spreading their fingers to fly.
Darkness grows their replacements—
as easily as a clock's minute-hand
falls down into,
crawls back out of
each hour's hole.

USE

A bird's beak. Re-curved,
de-curved, serrate, hooked.
Each to its purpose.
Dark, pale, honeyed, dun,
of use. Stabbing, probing, it keeps
its size, its shape, by balancing
constant growth and constant use.
A small and honed proof.

Onward it grows, fed by a heart's
swift little engine that's fed by
what the beak can dislodge.
Outward—against grit or bark—
it wears away as much of itself
as it adds. *The use of use*: to keep
a beak as beak, exactly.
Worn to perfection.

VOLUPTUARIES

The earth flicks, twirls
the feathery torque of its growth.
Evened spaces fall down, shatter,
scatter away, the ratchet of birdsong
repleting. To then pause, repeat.

Passing through what might be
inclined to throw down a shadow,
light becomes wings so yellow
they're breathless, blades
so quick and thin they sing.

Air shimmies outward, gold shinnies
up the trees. A perfume brews
for drinking—long gulps,
deep drafts. Liquor of pollen,
ester of want and plenty.

The weighty, suffusing, never-to-be-
satisfied. With vernal string
wafted from green, leaf-ladders
braid themselves up and into
the somewhere of blue.

AFTERWORD: THE COMING EVE DELICIOUS

Be not too certain but I
am now with you . . .

—*Walt Whitman (1860)*

Many lucky listeners who attend Paulann Petersen's poetry readings in the near future will gallivant into the night with answers to the questions: *Who are we?* and *What are we doing here?* ("Skin") They will walk with the poet on the ancient sands of Greek isles, the Bosporus, or the moon. The bravest of them might attend preparations for their own burials. ("To My Coffin Maker") They will visit blooming gardens, sacred groves, or a thrumming hive of bees about to explode in search of nectar. ("Hive") They will peer with the poet into blazing centers of natural beauty, and understand at last the force that is necessary for nurturing life on earth. ("Small Wonder," "Fig" and "Feeding Crows")

The heroine of *The Voluptuary* is not a king's sybaritic mistress, installed in the summer palace at Versailles. Her assignations are with the stars, with color and the air. ("Silver and Deep") The richness she is sifting with her mind has everything to do with the amplitude of the earth and the generosity of her interior self. ("Among the Yet Unfallen," "Gravity" and "Wax")

The companions who mostly comprise the human presence in the book are Whitmans all: Paulann Petersen *nee* Whitman; the poet's deceased parents, Grace and Paul Whitman, wearing their shrouds; and Walter Whitman Jr., himself, represented in his mythological sense as the Zeus of American poetry. The three specters are lovingly portrayed against a backdrop teeming with life, tracking events like illuminated planets in the intimate relationships of men, women, the moon, and the stars. They are characters in a play for whom a master painter or weaver has created a billowing meticulous stage set that rivals life in its most minute and fanciful details, ". . . the treasure," as Pablo Neruda once described it, "that we find inside a kernel of wheat," or what our author identifies as the "body of this world [in] its coat of wild color," the "hoarded blue of unopened song . . ."

The hoarded blue of unopened song—that's as good as any definition I've seen of the grail that poets seek, the electricity they crave, to animate their inner selves. It's a phrase that symbolizes the simultaneous coming together of time, location, and color—what mind and self have to inhabit in order to act, to stroll down the broad, tree-lined avenues of prosody together. Prosody, that holy grail, "all parts together," as Walt Whitman referred to it, which he tempered with the "coming eve delicious," the poetic equation that produces a sunset, a just-opened jar of honey, the gravitational pull of a crescent moon on the ark of the world.

Whitman's acolyte, having absorbed what she needed from the battle-scarred, magisterial old wizard, now reveals herself ready for full flight. From the profligate mentor, Walt Whitman: "The gentle soft-born measureless light . . ." From our living, breathing poet, Paulann Petersen: "The weighty, suffusing, never-to-be-satisfied . . ." the "feathery torque . . ." the *"anywhere* skin . . ."

The Voluptuary is vast; its pages define magnanimity. The contrasts within it are razor sharp—sun and moon, darkness and light, bumblebee and raven—all parts of life shot through with the silken strands of green, of grass in the fields and leaves on the trees, everything bathed in honeyed light. Paulann Petersen's poems read as if they are pieces from an "endless library," as she implies in her definition of poetry, something infinite and deep, like a well. She sees her words cast from a sounding-bowl across the sky, words as fine as "any line-up of suns a night sky could flaunt." Those worlds illuminate our path to the well. We lift our shining gourds and drink.

—*Greg Simon*
Portland, Oregon